North American Continent

Welcome to the exciting world of endangered animals in North America! North America is a big continent with lots of countries like the United States, Canada, Mexico, and many more! It has tall mountains, huge forests, beautiful deserts, and awesome beaches. You'll find incredible animals like majestic birds flying in the sky and magnificent mammals roaming the land. But some animals need our help because they're endangered. Endangered means they might disappear forever! In this coloring book, you'll meet these special creatures and learn fun facts about where they live, what they eat, and how many are left. So get your colored pencils ready and let's protect and save these amazing animals together!

North Atlantic Right Whale

The North Atlantic Right Whale is a huge ocean creature that lives in the cold Atlantic waters. They can grow up to 50 feet long and weigh around 70 tons! They have special blowholes on their heads for breathing. There are only about 400 left in the world. They eat tiny shrimp-like animals called zooplankton and use baleen plates in their mouths to filter food from the water. We must help protect these incredible whales from extinction!

California Condor

The California Condor is a large and impressive bird from California. It has a huge wingspan of about 9 feet! These birds were almost extinct, but thanks to conservation efforts, their population is slowly growing. Currently, there are around 400 California Condors in the wild. They eat dead animals, and scientists are working to breed them in captivity and release them back into the wild.

Mexican Gray Wolf

The Mexican Gray Wolf is a special and endangered animal from North America. It looks like a big gray dog with a bushy tail. There are currently around 150 Mexican Gray Wolves in the wild. They were almost extinct, but now their numbers are slowly growing. These wolves hunt elk and deer and live in packs.

Florida Manatee

The Florida Manatee is a gentle and endangered marine animal that lives in the warm waters of Florida. They are also known as "sea cows" because of their calm nature. Manatees can grow up to 10 to 12 feet long and weigh around 1,000 to 1,500 pounds! They eat plants like seagrass and algae. Sadly, there are approximately 6,500 Florida Manatees left in the world.

Hawaiian Monk Seal

The Hawaiian Monk Seal is a special and endangered marine mammal from the Hawaiian Islands. They have sleek bodies and big, round eyes. These amazing seals primarily feed on a variety of marine creatures such as fish, squid, and crustaceans. Sadly, there are only about 1,400 Hawaiian Monk Seals left in the world.

Ivory Billed Woodpecker

The Ivory-billed Woodpecker is a magnificent bird that used to live in the southeastern United States. It has beautiful black and white feathers and a bright red crest. Sadly, it is critically endangered, and there may be only a few, if any, left in the wild. These woodpeckers primarily eat insects found in dead or decaying trees.

Mississippi Gopher Frog

The Mississippi Gopher Frog is a special and endangered amphibian found in the southern United States. It has a plump body and dark spots. Unfortunately, there are only a few hundred Mississippi Gopher Frogs left in the world, making them critically endangered. They eat insects and small invertebrates, and they need clean habitats to survive.

Red Wolf

The Red Wolf is an endangered species of wolf found in the southeastern United States. They have a reddish-brown coat and are smaller than gray wolves. Sadly, there are only about 10 to 20 Red Wolves left in the wild. They eat small mammals like rabbits and rodents.

Leatherback Sea Turtle

The Leatherback Sea Turtle is the largest species of sea turtle, found in oceans near Florida, Puerto Rico, and Virgin Islands. They have a unique leathery shell and can grow over six feet long. Leatherbacks primarily eat jellyfish. Sadly, they are critically endangered, with only around 20,000 nesting females left.

Houston Toad

The Houston Toad is an endangered amphibian found in Texas. It is small, light brown or gray, and has dark spots. Sadly, there are only a few hundred Houston Toads left in the wild. They eat insects and other small invertebrates.

Sierra Nevada Bighorn Sheep

The Sierra Nevada Bighorn Sheep is an endangered species from the mountains of California. They have curved horns and there are only around 600 left in the world. These sheep are herbivores, meaning they eat plants like grasses, shrubs, and herbs. They are also excellent climbers and can scale steep cliffs with ease.

Florida Panther

The Florida Panther is a magnificent and endangered big cat that calls Florida its home. It is a subspecies of the mountain lion and is known for its beautiful tan coat and striking green eyes. Sadly, there are only around 120 to 230 Florida Panthers left in the wild, making them critically endangered. These panthers are carnivores, which means they eat meat. They primarily prey on animals like deer, hogs, and smaller mammals.

Whooping Crane

The Whooping Crane is a fascinating and endangered bird that is native to North America. It is one of the tallest birds in North America, standing about five feet tall! There are only around 600 Whooping Cranes left in the world. These cranes eat a variety of foods including insects, small fish, frogs, and plants. They have a distinct call that sounds like a whooping sound, hence their name.

Indiana Bat

The Indiana Bat is a fascinating and endangered species of bat found in the United States. They are small, with a wingspan of about nine inches! There are only around 400,000 Indiana Bats left in the world. These bats are insectivores, meaning they eat insects like moths, beetles, and mosquitoes. Indiana Bats hibernate in caves during winter and migrate to different areas for summer.

Black-footed Ferret

The Black-footed Ferret is a remarkable and endangered animal native to North America. It is known for its unique markings and black feet. There are only around 300 Black-footed Ferrets left in the wild. These ferrets are carnivores and mainly eat small animals like prairie dogs. They are excellent hunters and have sharp teeth and claws.

Hawaiian Crow

The Hawaiian Crow, also known as the 'Alalā, is a special and critically endangered bird from Hawaii. It is known for its glossy black feathers and strong beak. There are currently fewer than 200 Hawaiian Crows left in the world. They eat a varied diet that includes fruits, insects, and even small vertebrates. The 'Alalā is highly intelligent and known for its problem-solving abilities.

Puerto Rican Parrot

The Puerto Rican Parrot is a captivating and endangered bird native to Puerto Rico. It has beautiful green feathers and a colorful beak. There are only around 200 Puerto Rican Parrots left in the wild. These parrots are herbivores, which means they eat fruits, nuts, seeds, and flowers. They are excellent fliers and can be seen soaring through the forests of Puerto Rico.

Alabama Beach Mouse

The Alabama Beach Mouse lives along the sandy beaches of Alabama. It is a small mouse with soft brown fur and big, round eyes. There are only about 300 Alabama Beach Mice left in the world. These mice have a specialized diet and primarily eat seeds, fruits, and insects. They are excellent burrowers and create tunnels in the sand dunes where they live.

Piping Plover

The Piping Plover is a charming and endangered bird that lives along sandy beaches and shorelines in North America. These small birds have a pale brownish color with white underparts and distinctive black bands on their necks. There are approximately 8,000 Piping Plovers left in the world. Piping Plovers eat a variety of small insects and invertebrates found in the sand and shallow water.

California Tiger Salamander

The California Tiger Salamander is a captivating amphibian from California. It has striking yellow and black markings like a tiger. Sadly, there are only a few thousand left in the world, making them endangered. They eat insects, worms, and small fish.

San Joaquin Kit Fox

The San Joaquin Kit Fox is a captivating and endangered fox found in California's San Joaquin Valley. It has a sandy brown coat and big ears. Sadly, there are only a few thousand left in the world, making them critically endangered. They eat small mammals, birds, insects, and even fruits and vegetables.

Mount Graham Red Squirrel

The Mount Graham Red Squirrel is a unique and endangered creature found in the forests of Mount Graham in Arizona. It has a vibrant red coat and a bushy tail. Sadly, there are only a few hundred Mount Graham Red Squirrels left in the world, making them critically endangered. These squirrels have a diverse diet and eat a variety of foods including pine cones, seeds, nuts, and sometimes insects.

Oregon Silverspot Butterfly

The Oregon Silverspot Butterfly is a beautiful and endangered species that lives in the coastal areas of Oregon, USA. It has stunning orange wings with silver spots. Sadly, there are only a few hundred Oregon Silverspot Butterflies left in the world, making them critically endangered. These butterflies have a special diet and primarily eat a specific plant called the early blue violet.

Columbia Basin Pygmy Rabbit

The Columbia Basin Pygmy Rabbit is one of the smallest rabbit species, measuring only about 9 inches in length that lives in the Columbia Basin of Washington, USA. There are only around 200 Columbia Basin Pygmy Rabbits left in the wild. These rabbits primarily eat sagebrush, which is their main source of food and shelter. They are excellent burrowers and create tunnels to hide from predators.

Guatemalan Black Howler Monkey

The Guatemalan Black Howler Monkey is found in the forests of Guatemala. They are known for their jet-black fur and long tail, which helps them swing from tree to tree. There are only around 200 Guatemalan Black Howler Monkeys left in the world. These monkeys are herbivores, meaning they eat a variety of fruits, leaves, and flowers found in the forest.

Cuban Crocodile

The Cuban Crocodile is an amazing reptile that lives in the beautiful island of Cuba. It is known for its striking green color and sharp teeth. Sadly, there are only around 3,000 Cuban Crocodiles left in the wild, making them a critically endangered species. These crocodiles are carnivores, which means they eat meat. They mainly hunt fish, birds, and small mammals that come near the water's edge.

Trinidad Piping Guan

The Trinidad Piping Guan lives in the forests of Trinidad and Tobago. It is known for its beautiful feathers and unique call that sounds like a piping flute! Sadly, there are only around 250 Trinidad Piping Guans left in the world, making them critically endangered. These birds eat fruits, seeds, and insects found in the forest. They are excellent fliers and can soar gracefully through the trees.

www.ingramcontent.com/pod-product-compliance
Lightning Source LLC
Chambersburg PA
CBHW080044260726
48658CB00007B/2733